HIP-HOP

Alicia Keys	Lil Wayne
Ashanti	LL Cool J
Beyoncé	Lloyd Banks
Black Eyed Peas	Ludacris
Busta Rhymes	Mariah Carey
Chris Brown	Mary J. Blige
Christina Aguilera	Missy Elliot
Ciara	Nas
Cypress Hill	Nelly
Daddy Yankee	Notorious B.I.G.
DMX	OutKast
Don Omar	Pharrell Williams
Dr. Dre	Pitbull
Eminem	Queen Latifah
Fat Joe	Reverend Run (of Run DMC)
50 Cent	Sean "Diddy" Combs
The Game	Snoop Dogg
Hip-Hop: A Short History	T.I.
Hip-Hop Around the World	Tupac
Ice Cube	Usher
Ivy Queen	Will Smith
Jay-Z	Wu-Tang Clan
Jennifer Lopez	Xzibit
Juelz Santana	Young Jeezy
Kanye West	Yung Joc

From a Disney Mouseketeer to glamorous musician, Christina Aguilera has become one of the biggest names in the music world.

Christina Aguilera

MaryJo Lemmens

Mason Crest Publishers

Christina Aguilera

Produced by Harding House Publishing Service, Inc.
201 Harding Avenue, Vestal, NY 13850.

MASON CREST PUBLISHERS INC.
370 Reed Road
Broomall, Pennsylvania 19008
(866)MCP-BOOK (toll free)
www.masoncrest.com

Printed in the United States of America

First Printing

9 8 7 6 5 4 3 2 1

Library of Congress Cataloging-in-Publication Data

Lemmens, MaryJo.
  Christina Aguilera / MaryJo Lemmens.
     p. cm. — (Hip-hop)
  Includes bibliographical references and index.
  ISBN 978-1-4222-0285-2
  ISBN: 978-1-4222-0077-3 (series)
  1. Aguilera, Christina, 1980—Juvenile literature. 2. Singers—United States—Bi-
ography—Juvenile literature. I. Title.
  ML3930.A36L46 2008
  782.42164092—dc22
  [B]
                              2007028094

Publisher's notes:
• All quotations in this book come from original sources and contain the spell-
  ing and grammatical inconsistencies of the original text.

• The Web sites mentioned in this book were active at the time of publication. The publisher is not responsible for Web sites that have changed their
  addresses or discontinued operation since the date of publication. The
  publisher will review and update the Web site addresses each time the book
  is reprinted.

DISCLAIMER: The following story has been thoroughly researched, and to the
best of our knowledge, represents a true story. While every possible effort
has been made to ensure accuracy, the publisher will not assume liability for
damages caused by inaccuracies in the data, and makes no warranty on the
accuracy of the information contained herein. This story has not been
authorized nor endorsed by Christina Aguilera.

Contents

Hip-Hop Time Line

1970s DJ Kool Herc pioneers the use of breaks, isolations, and repeats using two turn-tables.

1976 Grandmaster Flash and the Furious Five emerge as one of the first battlers and freestylers.

1984 The track "Roxanne Roxanne" sparks the first diss war.

1982 Afrika Bambaataa tours Europe in another hip-hop first.

1988 Hip-hop record sales reach 100 million annually.

1970s Grafitti artist Vic begins tagging on New York subways.

1980 Rapper Kurtis Blow sells a million records and makes the first nationwide TV appearance for a hip-hop artist.

1985 The film *Krush Groove*, about the rise of Def Jam Records, is released.

1970   1980

1970s The central elements of the hip-hop culture begin to emerge in the Bronx, New York City.

1983 Ice-T releases his first singles, marking the earliest examples of gangsta rap.

1986 Run DMC cover Aerosmith's "Walk this Way" and appear on the cover of *Rolling Stone*.

1979 "Rapper's Delight," by The Sugarhill Gang, goes gold.

1974 Afrika Bambaataa organizes the Universal Zulu Nation.

1984 *Graffitti Rock*, the first hip-hop television program, premieres.

1981 Grandmaster Flash and the Furious Five release *Adventures on the Wheels of Steel*.

1988 MTV premieres *Yo! MTV Raps*.

1989 *Billboard* recognizes rap music as a category.

1993 Snoop Dogg's debut album *Doggystyle* becomes the first hip-hop album to debut at #1.

2003 50 Cent debuts with *Get Rich or Die Tryin*.

2006 The Smithsonian National Museum of American History announces the creation of a new hip-hop exhibition, scheduled to open in two years.

1997 The Notorious B.I.G. is gunned down in Los Angeles.

1990s Hip-hop gains popularity in Europe.

2007 Grandmaster Flash and the Furious Five are the first rap artists to be inducted into the Rock and Roll Hall of Fame.

1994 Nas releases *Illmatic*, which becomes the first album to ever receive a five out of five rating from *The Source*.

2004 The first National Hip-Hop Political Convention is held in New Jersey.

1990   2000

1994 In Puerto Rico, the musical genre that had been called "Dem Bow" or "Underground" now starts to be referred to as "Reggaeton."

2004 Daddy Yankee's single "Gasolina" rockets into mainstream popularity in the US, marking the rise of reggaeton in the US.

1990 In Puerto Rico, DJs inspired by Panamanian reggae begin to produce their own music.

1996 Tupac Shakur is killed in Las Vegas.

2003 For the first time, the top ten artists on the *Billboard* charts are all African American. Notably, they are all part of the Dirty South.

1992 DJ Playero releases his mixtape *32*, which has some of the earliest examples of reggaeton recorded, including a track by Daddy Yankee.

2001 Russell Simmons founds the Hip-hop Action Network.

2007 Numerous hip-hop artists perform at the Live Earth concerts, which take place around the globe.

The 2007 Grammy Awards ceremony saw a cool, calm, collected, and very glamorous Christina Aguilera take home a statue. She was a big star, and she looked every inch the part.

Top of the
Charts

Fans cheered, fellow musicians applauded, and record industry executives nodded their approval. All across the world, millions of people had their televisions tuned to the live event: the 2007 Grammy Awards. They watched as Christina Aguilera stepped on stage and claimed the award for Best Female Pop Vocal Performance. It wasn't her first Grammy, but it was significant nonetheless. After years of intense public scrutiny, media criticism, and controversy, Christina, looking poised and mature, claimed the award that proved she was a real artist.

The Real Deal

In the popular music world, there are all types of singers. Plenty have become famous more for their looks, personalities, and stylish packaging than any true vocal ability. Not Christina Aguilera.

She is of course beautiful, with a personality and style that draw attention, but it is her singing that sets her apart from other pop stars. She has an unforgettable range and a deep, sultry, powerful voice that seems impossible for her petite size. Unlike so many other female pop artists, for Christina the spectacle and image of celebrity could easily take a backseat to her talents as a naturally gifted singer.

Even with undisputed vocal abilities, however, Christina's career has been controversial. While she is a great singer, many people know her for her provocative image, sexual songs, and explicit videos first and for her talent second. Since her career took off, Christina has been a music journalist's dream come true, always providing something explosive for the entertainment media's front pages.

On the day she accepted her 2007 Grammy Award, however, it was not a controversial Christina Aguilera who took the stage; it was Christina the singer—the one who effortlessly glides from 1920s **blues** to Broadway-inspired pop songs, from a soulful 1960s ballad to the pumping hip-hop of the new millennium. This is the Christina who can walk on stage in a 1950s dress and hairstyle and make it look as youthful and modern as she is. The woman on stage at the 2007 Grammy Awards was the Christina who wows and inspires audiences all over the world.

The Hip-Hop Influence

Christina Aguilera is part of a whole generation of performers who have been heavily influenced by hip-hop music and culture. Hip-hop is a style of music that began with New York City's African American and Latino communities in the Bronx in the 1970s. It all started at the dance parties that were popular in clubs, on the streets, and even in the parks; parties where DJs would often hotwire streetlights to get the power for their equipment. Life in the Bronx was hard, with poverty and crime seemingly around every corner. People didn't have

Hip-hop is all about dance. The goal is to get people up on the dance floor and to keep them there—dancing the night away.

much, and block parties, music, and dancing were ways to escape and find joy in an otherwise difficult life.

Hip-hop was born when DJs began manipulating records to make the music more danceable. They did it by setting up two turntables, isolating the breaks (or beat-driven part of a song), and then mixing back and forth between the records, splicing the breaks together and allowing partiers to dance on and on. The technique caught on fast, and DJs elevated spinning records into an art form.

DJs were the stars of early hip-hop. Skill in scratching and mixing could make a DJ famous. Today, technology has taken over many of the tasks originated by the pioneering DJs.

Rapping was the next musical innovation. Some of the DJs worked the mic while they spun records, shouting out to the partiers, telling jokes, saying anything to keep people interested and entertained. It was called emceeing (or MCing), and soon MCs became separate from the DJs, developing their own art form based on rhythm and rhyme. The style became known as rapping. Over the years rap became increasingly complex, and eventually rappers overtook DJs as the stars of hip-hop music.

The hip-hop music that developed from these efforts was the raw, gritty music of the urban ghetto. It was born in the Bronx, especially the South Bronx, a place seething with discontent, poverty, and crime, but it didn't stay there for long. It spread first across New York and then to other cities throughout America. At every stop, the music inspired the young people living in the country's toughest streets. From there it went to urban radio stations, then **mainstream** stations, and finally it hit the ears of the world.

Hip-hop grabs you and doesn't let go. The beat gets into your body, the rhymes get into your brain, and you want to *be* the music. You want to jump to it, rap with it, throw your fist up in the air and be **defiant**. It's alive and real, and it moves your soul. The pumping music raises you up, entertains you, inspires you; it allows you to escape and, for a moment, be something different. It is the harsh music of the inner city and the hopeful expression of people's dreams. This music clawed its way out of the ghetto, overcame color lines and class barriers, and became some of the most popular music on earth.

Hip-hop music and culture have influenced music, dance, fashion, and even language all over the world. Once the music of urban black and Latino youths, hip-hop has become a music for all people. It is the new cultural language of young people, and hip-hop fans can relate to each other even if they come from very different backgrounds. For perhaps the first time in history, a poor kid in the inner city is listening to the same music as an upper-class kid in Beverly Hills. And the hip-hop revolution has even spread around the world, linking fans in the United States with fans in Asia, Europe, the Middle East, and elsewhere.

Today, artists from many backgrounds are influenced by hip-hop's sound. Popular artists like Christina Aguilera show hip-hop influences in their music, dance, and stage images. Female artists like Christina have also taken hip-hop (once

For much of hip-hop's history, it was a man's game. Few women were able to find success in the genre. That wouldn't last, though. Women such as Christina eventually made their mark in hip-hop.

the nearly exclusive domain of male artists) and claimed it, bringing it into their music and giving it a new style of their own. In return, hip-hop flavors have helped make artists like Christina some of the most popular performers around.

No Boundaries

In just under ten years in the popular music industry, Christina Aguilera has reinvented herself many times. She's been a sweet Mouseketeer; a teen idol; a naughty, shameless sex symbol; and a sultry, classy vixen. Her music also defies definition. Her music is pop, *R&B*, hip-hop, dance, Latin, and even *soul*, blues, and *jazz*. She's been many things, sung in many styles, and fought through many controversies, all the while using her extreme vocal muscle to keep her at the top of the charts.

In the time it takes most people to graduate high school, go to college, and start their first career, Christina Aguilera has become an international singing sensation, released five albums, sold approximately thirty million copies globally, earned sixteen Grammy nominations, and claimed five Grammy Awards. She has also grown up in the public eye, gotten married, evolved into a talented songwriter and successful producer, and become one of the richest women in show business. Not bad for someone who isn't even thirty years old.

As good as things are for Christina now, however, life wasn't always bright lights and joyful stardom. Christina has suffered hard times and career highs and lows. She's faced the challenge of growing up under intense media scrutiny, and when she's stumbled (as all people sometimes do), cameras and critics have been there to document and comment on every wrong move. Christina will be the first to tell you that she loves her work and thinks she has the greatest job in the world, but she'll also be the first to say that it's a hard job that comes with sacrifices. Every record has its B-side, and Christina has had her fair share of fame's hard knocks.

Christina Aguilera may be tiny in stature, but her voice is huge. She's learned how to use her voice to bring out the best in the songs she sings—no matter what style.

The Little Girl with the Big Voice

Christina Aguilera was born on December 18, 1980, on Staten Island in New York City. New York is known for its *diversity*. People from many different backgrounds and parts of the world live in the city. Their cultures, beliefs, and art forms influence and inspire each other, blending and changing to become things that are new and unique. In a way, however, the area where Christina was born was far from the typical mix on New York City's streets. Staten Island is mostly suburban, and compared to the vibrant, multicultural city that surrounds it, Staten Island is not nearly as diverse.

Christina, however, needed to look no further than her own home to find a fertile mix of cultures. Her father is Latino. He was born in the South American country of Ecuador. Her Irish American mother was a Spanish-language teacher. As a child, Spanish was commonly spoken in Christina's home. Although her parents later divorced and she became estranged from her father, her Latino heritage remains important to her and influences her music.

When a child's domestic life is shattered by anger, the scars can last a lifetime. Despite Christina's scars, she has proven a person can rise above her past.

The Early Years

In addition to teaching Spanish, Christina's mother was a talented piano and violin player, so Christina was surrounded and inspired by music early on. She also traveled from a very early age. Her father, Fausto Wagner Xavier Aguilera, was a U.S. Army sergeant. As a member of a military family, Christina found herself moving around the world as her father was posted to different American bases. She spent time living in Texas and in Canada and Japan.

Military life was difficult. The frequent moves created upheaval, and it was difficult for Christina to have close friends when she moved so often. Her father's aggressive and controlling behavior also strained the family. In interviews, Christina has said that he was abusive. She has also stated that, in her experience, domestic violence was quite common on military bases, and there were few support systems families could turn to for real help. In an interview with Jenny Eliscu for *USA Weekend* magazine, she explained that domestic violence was an all-too common part of her childhood:

> *"It happens to so many people. My father was a sergeant in the Army, so we lived on Army bases when I was little, and it [domestic violence] was happening a lot. The MPs [military police] would come, but a lot of them were doing the same things [to their wives and kids]. I was surrounded with domestic violence, not only in my home but my friends'."*

When Christina was seven years old, her parents divorced. Her mother took Christina and her younger sister, Rachel. They moved to Christina's grandmother's house in a suburb of Pittsburgh, Pennsylvania. In recent years, Christina's father has indicated his desire to reconcile with his daughter, but Christina has not agreed to it.

Her troubled relationship with her father and her parents' divorce left lasting impressions on Christina. The unhappiness and emotional damage from her childhood continued to affect her many years later. In songs like "I'm OK" and "Oh Mother," she talks about those years and their lasting effects. In the chorus of "I'm OK," she sings to an abusive father about the hurt he has caused:

"Bruises fade father, but the pain remains the same
And I still remember how you kept me so afraid"

In "Oh Mother," Christina sings of a woman who thinks she's found the perfect man, only to be caught in an abusive relationship. She stays with him until he turns on their children. Then she knows she must leave to save her kids. In the song, Christina thanks that mother for all of her sacrifices.

Baby Steps in the Mouse's Shadow

In those early years in Pennsylvania, Christina turned to music to express her emotions and transform her life. She loved the musical *The Sound of Music*. Like other girls her age, Christina also listened to popular artists like Madonna and Whitney Houston. But she idolized artists from an older generation as well, singers like Billie Holiday, Aretha Franklin, and Etta James. While her friends were dancing to the newest pop and rock, Christina danced to blues, soul, and jazz.

Christina sang and performed every chance she had, and soon she became known as "the little girl with the big voice" around her neighborhood. But Christina's talent was not well received by everyone, and she struggled for acceptance. When Christina began winning all the local talent shows and singing competitions others became jealous. Her fellow competitors would back out of competitions if they learned that Christina

The New Mickey Mouse Club provided many young stars with their first taste of national success. Britney Spears, Christina, and Justin Timberlake all came to national attention on the show.

would be singing. In interviews, Christina has explained that other kids her age often didn't understand her interests and ambitions. Sometimes they believed that she was full of herself and thought she was better than them. (Christina has said nothing could have been further from the truth.) She was even sometimes bullied. At one point, she had to switch schools, and from then on, she tried to keep her singing and talent quiet around other kids.

But Christina's talent was undeniable. And her energy was infectious. Like a gathering storm, people soon began to notice this young woman emerging on pop's horizon. At the age of ten, she appeared on *Star Search*, singing "A Sunday Kind of Love" by Etta James. She lost the competition, but caught plenty of people's eyes and ears. She appeared on KDKA-TV, a local station, to perform the song on the air a second time.

She also began performing in front of larger audiences. She sang "The Star-Spangled Banner" before Pittsburgh Penguins hockey games, Steelers football games, and Pirates baseball games. Then came her first big-league break. It was 1993, and she was selected as a Mouseketeer for *The New Mickey Mouse Club* on the Disney Channel. Her costars would become a who's who of today's largest pop stars; Britney Spears, Justin Timberlake, and JC Chasez all took a turn working for "the Mouse." Christina, one of the youngest of the group, became known among her 'tween co-stars as something of a **diva**.

Some people claim Christina (and other young stars like her) has been forced into the public eye by overbearing stage parents desperate for attention and fame. Christina says, for her, this was never the case. In an interview with Evelyn McDonnell, Christina said that, although her mother and grandmother recognized her talent, she was the driving force behind her early career:

"My mom was definitely behind me 100 percent, but really it was my grandma who noticed something was

different about me. When I played, I would spread towels on the floor as my stage and use my mom's old twirling baton as my microphone. If anything, I pushed my mom. Everything I've gotten just fell into my lap. I had no acting experience or vocal training when I auditioned for The Mickey Mouse Club."

Christina's self-titled debut album was a smash hit all over the world. She was no longer known just as a former Mouseketeer; though only nineteen, she had grown into a music phenomenon. And she had a Grammy to prove it.

Promising as it was, her time in Mickey's shadow was short lived. The show was cancelled in 1994. Christina took the cancellation as an opportunity to try to land something bigger and more permanent.

Pop Goes Christina

Hungering for a record deal, Christina began cutting **demo** tapes. At fourteen years old, Christina recorded "All I Wanna Do" with Keizo Nakanishi, a Japanese singer. Soon afterward, she appeared in Romania at the Golden Stag Festival, which features appearances by both Romanian and international stars.

Romania, a small country in Eastern Europe, may seem a world away from the American popular music scene. Over the years, however, the Golden Stag Festival has hosted some of the biggest names in American music. Ray Charles, Sheryl Crow, INXS, Kenny Rogers, and many more have performed at the Golden Stag, and Christina's appearance there was a hint that she was a rising star.

That faintly glimmering, rising star was about to go super-nova. Christina was hunting for a record deal. She recorded a demo tape in her bathroom, and the homemade recording once again brought the teenager to Disney's attention. Disney was working on its newest full-length animated feature, *Mulan*, and as soon as they heard Christina's tape, they knew they wanted the young teen for the soundtrack. Christina became the voice of "Reflection," and the song launched her popular music career. Within days of recording the song, Christina landed her first record contract.

In 1999, Christina exploded onto the pop scene with her first album. Titled simply *Christina Aguilera*, it slammed onto the charts, debuting at #1 on the *Billboard* 200. The singles "Genie in a Bottle," "What a Girl Wants," and "Come on Over Baby (All I Want is You)" became #1 hits on the *Billboard* Hot 100. In less than a year, the album went six-times **platinum**, selling more the six million copies in the United States alone. It would eventually sell millions more worldwide.

Christina's first album made her an instant star around the world. Suddenly her name and face were everywhere, and her voice was in everyone's ears. Her work received three nominations at the 2000 Grammy Awards, and she beat out Macy Gray, Kid Rock, Susan Tedeschi, and Britney Spears (who was widely expected to win) to be named Best New Artist of the year. She was just nineteen years old.

Christina's appearance on the music scene was part of a "pop princess" craze. Britney Spears, Christina Aguilera, Jessica Simpson, and Mandy Moore all launched their first albums within months of each other. They instantaneously won both fans and critics. While fans loved their danceable tunes and cover-girl looks, critics called their music "bubble-gum pop"—music created by record-industry executives to sell, but that has no real artistic value or creativity. Christina wouldn't be satisfied with an image like that for long.

With her first success, Christina Aguilera was lumped into a category called "bubblegum pop" by many music critics. That made the young artist cringe. She wanted to be taken seriously, and she was willing to do whatever it took to break from that label.

3

Bubblegum Sweet to Heavy Heat

Christina's sudden success was exciting, a dream come true, but she wasn't totally satisfied. She didn't want people to know her as a bubblegum pop princess. She wanted them to know her as a great singer and artist; she wanted to be taken seriously as a musician. The songs on her first album, however, didn't really give her a lot of opportunity to show her real vocal ability. Furthermore, her newfound success wasn't always easy. She did an interview with Evelyn McDonnell at that time and talked about the difficulties of being a teen star: being isolated from peers, having to grow up fast, and struggling for control over the music:

"I had a few friends, but they would want to rant and rave and go off about boys, and I'd want to talk careers. You

Self-absorbed, pushy, not always a pleasant person to be around; those were just some of the ways people described Christina. She agrees that those adjectives were sometimes true, but it wasn't because she was trying to be difficult; she was just working too hard.

grow up so much faster in the business, so it's really tough to be nineteen, to be female, and to go up against your record company heads, who have their own perception of what you should be, what you should like, what you should sound like. You have to be that much stronger than someone older. I feel like a 35-year-old business woman in a nineteen-year-old body."

As Christina's popularity grew, so did her image. And that image wasn't always positive. People began calling her a diva, saying she was self-absorbed and pushy. In an interview with *Allure*, Christina admitted that there were times when she probably wasn't the most pleasant person in the world, but that it all came from being pushed too hard and having every moment of her time scheduled by other people:

"For a while it was to the point that I was losing my voice and I thought I was going to have to be hospitalized if I kept working myself into the ground. I ended up getting really introverted. I wasn't happy. But nobody knows what's really going on. I need to eat, I need to sleep, and sometimes those things weren't considered. It was like, 'When do you think I'll have time to go to the bathroom?' That wasn't on the schedule."

First Love

The period after Christina's first album, however, certainly wasn't all negative. There was also a lot of joy to be found in her new fame and in exploring herself as a maturing person. Perhaps the best part was falling in love for the first time. As she explained in her *Allure* interview, she didn't really think love would happen for her. In fact, because of her past, she didn't even want it to happen to her:

"I'm very career-oriented, plus I have vulnerability issues. My mom went through a really bad marriage, and seeing that hurt me. I thought, 'I'm never going to let a man do that to me.' I thought of being in a relationship as being weak."

But, unexpectedly, love did come her way, blossoming with one of her dancers while she was on tour. His name was Jorge, and as Christina explained to *Allure*, being with him made her see that being in love could be a wonderful thing:

"But then when my relationship with Jorge happened, I wanted to give, I wanted to be there. I'd never even had a huge crush on a guy before. Then it just happened, on tour. We were dancing together, spending a lot of time together, and we fell in love."

The love didn't last, but for Christina, it was still something wonderful that helped her grow and mature as a person and as a woman. Unlike many loves that end, Christina and Jorge were able to remain friends. She told *Allure* that they continue to work together, respect one another, and cherish what they had:

"Even though we're not together anymore, we still work together. He's a really great person. And I love him."

Searching for Herself

Christina was maturing and gaining more control over her emotional life. It wasn't long before she began exerting more creative control over her work as well. She started by embracing her Latin roots, creating a Spanish-language album called *Mi Reflejo*. Although she didn't speak Spanish fluently, she found that the introduction she'd had to Spanish in her early childhood made it easier to get a handle on the language and sing the songs with authenticity. The album, which was released in September 2000, was embraced by much of the Latino community, going on to win a Latin Grammy Award for Best Female Pop Vocal Album in 2001. Christina was also named best-selling Latin artist at the World Music Awards.

Christina, although only half Latino, became part of a huge Latin craze in the popular music industry. There was a time

Christina's homage to her Latin roots with *Mi Reflejo* was a success. She won a Latin Grammy and a World Music Award for the album.

when being Latino in America's music industry or Hollywood was not considered a good thing, and many performers (if they wanted to appeal to America's larger, mostly white audience) took English-sounding stage names. The trend didn't just affect Latino performers. People of all different backgrounds adopted English-sounding names. Sometimes they simply wanted their names to be easier for most Americans to pronounce. Sometimes they hoped to hide their ethnic roots entirely. Rumor even has it that Christina herself was asked to drop her last name by record executives, something that (if the rumors are true) she obviously refused to do.

For many years, names like Lopez, Aguilera, Iglesias, and Estefan wouldn't have sat well with white audiences. Not so today. American music has experienced a "Latin explosion," and Latin pop and its artists are popular, not just with Spanish-speaking audiences, but with audiences of all backgrounds and all over the world. When Christina released her Spanish album, some people criticized her, saying she was simply trying to cash in on the Latin market. Christina, however, denounced such claims, saying that her Latino background is a legitimate and significant part of her heritage that she embraces and hopes to explore further.

A month after *Mi Reflejo* hit store shelves, Christina released a Christmas album, *My Kind of Christmas*. It sold well, but some critics claimed that Christina was oversinging. In interviews, Christina has been very candid about this problem, saying that a lot of her early work was indeed affected by her desire to show people that she had real vocal ability and could hit high notes. She said she was still struggling to break away from the canned, studio music being thrown at her and prove she could do more.

The public's first clue of the "more" came in 2001, when Christina, Lil' Kim, Mya, and Pink collaborated on the single "Lady Marmalade" for the movie *Moulin Rouge!* It was an instant hit, but it was definitely not what people had come to

Christina seemed to change her look as often as most people change socks. Her hair color changed, her makeup changed, and the way she dressed changed. Critics and fans were not always pleased with the result.

expect from the young pop star. Instead of her usual jeans and tummy-revealing crop-tops, Christina sported lingerie and heavy makeup for the music video. The lyrics too had shock value. The chorus, "*Voulez-vous coucher avec moi (ce soir)?*" is French for "Do you want to sleep with me tonight?" The song was an ultra-sexy remake of Patti LaBelle's 1975 hit, and it hinted of the new Christina who was waiting in the wings. Christina's second full-length English album was on the way, and she told *Time* magazine that it wouldn't be like the first:

> *"For me, in my heart, I have to move away from [teen pop]. Even if the label said I had to make another record like that, I don't think I could. Getting older, you just don't want to sing fluffy. You just have more things to say about real life and real people."*

Getting Hot and Heavy

In October 2002, *Stripped*, the much-anticipated follow-up to her first album, hit the record stores and caused an immediate sensation. The album had a tougher sound than fans previously heard from the blond starlet. In an interview with MTV, Christina said that her choice to go urban and edgier worried her producers, but as far as she was concerned, it was non-negotiable:

> *"I just get really bored with sticking to the norm and having the proper conservative image. That's just so not me. When 'Lady Marmalade' came out, so many executives were like, 'She can't do this.' 'It's too Rockwilder and Missy.' 'It's too urban.' And I was like, 'I'm doing it.' Even with certain outfits that I wear, or speaking openly about my past. I'm not going to sit there and lie. Whether you like me or hate me, that's me."*

Christina cowrote a lot of the material for her second album, showing that her talents go far beyond her voice. But her vocal and writing abilities weren't what grabbed people's attention this time around. People had far more to say about Christina's new image than her new sound. Christina emerged from the cocoon of her bubblegum phase sporting skimpy clothes, leather, several piercings, black hair, and a tattoo of her new nickname, "Xtina." The video for the first single, "Dirrty," was very sexual and equally controversial. Christina's new dirty-girl image caused a perhaps unexpected backlash.

In America, one thing is certain: sex sells. In the past, some musical artists' sent their careers into the stratosphere with sexual imagery and controversy. In the 1980s and '90s, Madonna, one of Christina's earliest music idols, was the poster child for the bad-girl image. Her music and videos were banned all over the world for their in-your-face sexuality and controversial subjects and images. The backlash certainly never hurt Madonna. In fact, it propelled her fame. It definitely kept all eyes on her, the media glued to her, and everyone guessing what she'd do next. More than that, it put Madonna at the forefront of her craft, making her a trendsetter and bringing her wide recognition as one of the bravest and most cutting-edge artists of her generation. It would probably have been reasonable for Christina to believe that an adult-image make-over would do the same for her.

The Backlash

Things did not work the same for Christina as they had for Madonna. People criticized Christina's new attitude and look, saying it was "raunchy," "dirty," and "in poor taste." It had been her decision to release "Dirrty" (and the shocking video) as the first single off the album. Her label wanted her to release the positive-messaged "Beautiful." "Dirrty" and the album started well on the charts, but sales quickly headed into a tailspin. The label rushed to release "Beautiful" to save sales and turn around the mini disaster. It seemed clear that a lot of fans still liked the old Christina of jeans, crop-tops, and good-girl looks and weren't ready to follow her into writhing videos and leather thongs.

The difference between Madonna and Christina's new image was that Madonna often used sexual imagery as part of a larger social or political theme. Madonna's pushing limits and boundaries was often a social or political commentary. At its best, her bad-girl image wasn't just about sex; it was about strength, power, equality, and breaking free of social, political, and religious constraints that limit people's abilities and realization of themselves. Certainly not everyone saw Madonna this way, but the fact that her music and **persona** has stood the test of time supports the idea that her work had a broader message and was about more than just explicit sexuality.

In talking about her new image and sexual videos, Christina made the same claims. She said that people were overlooking the fact that her "Dirrty" video showed a woman who, though scantily clad and free in her sexuality, was in the power position, taking control, doing only what she wanted to do, not what men told her to do. She told *People* magazine that the woman in the video was an **empowered** woman:

> *"I may have been the [scantily clad] girl in the video, but if you look at it carefully, I'm also at the forefront. I'm not just some lame chick in a rap video; I'm in the power position, in complete command of everything around me."*

Christina maintained that if people looked beyond the shocking imagery, they would see that her message was about being powerful and in control, feeling free to be oneself and explore one's hidden personality and desires without fear.

The media and many of Christina's fans, however, didn't buy it. A lot of the backlash was due to the fact that, at the beginning of her career, Christina was largely marketed to a young audience. Young girls worshipped singers like Christina, Britney Spears, and other pop princesses. Now Christina was accused of being irresponsible with her fame and sending the wrong messages to her younger fans, fans who liked to dress and behave like their favorite stars. Christina was getting heat from every angle, and it looked like it might seriously damage her career.

If Christina's goal was to change her image, it worked. As her clothes got skimpier and her music got tougher, fans and critics took notice. Her days as a bubblegum pop artist were over.

Christina Aguilera's edgier image wasn't the end of the story of her makeover. She glammed—and she grew up. Many people failed to realize that she hadn't had the chance to experiment in private like most people do as they grow up.

4

Free to Be Herself

Stripped grabbed everyone's attention, though probably not in the way Christina and the record company had hoped. The media was all over Christina, and even many of her fellow musicians criticized the new direction of her videos, her looks, and her career. But Christina didn't stumble under the pressure, and she didn't get caught up in self-doubt. The more she talked about what she was going through, the more it seemed like she knew what she was doing: pushing the envelope, perhaps a little too far, but doing so to grow up and establish herself as a formidable adult in the industry.

Christina Fights Back

Christina responded to the criticisms by saying that, while she recognized her role in the public eye and would do her best to behave responsibly in her daily life, she also needed to be true to herself. She needed the freedom to push the boundaries in her music, and if that meant sometimes she would push too hard, so be it. If people were looking for a squeaky clean role model who would always be the perfect "good girl," they were looking in the wrong place. Christina was firm; she wasn't in the business of being a perfect role model. She was in the business of being a cutting-edge performer.

Christina also pointed out that although some of her fans might be young girls, she was not. She had now left her teen years behind and was becoming a woman. She stated that while her peers were able to go off to college, explore themselves, and test their boundaries, she would have to do the same. Unfortunately for her, that would all happen in the public eye. Nevertheless, Christina saw her new image and sexual explorations as appropriate for her age and stage of life. She added an exclamation point to her statements by posing nude on the cover of *Rolling Stone* magazine and topless on the cover of *Maxim* magazine. She later created an even bigger stir when she and Britney Spears kissed Madonna in a performance for the MTV Video Music Awards.

The news for *Stripped*, however, wasn't all bad. Not by any means. In the end, beneath the sexual imagery and controversy, the music was much more solid and skillful than Christina's first album. All the negative **hype** prevented some people from seeing the album's artistic merits, but not everyone. Music mogul and famous *American Idol* judge Simon Cowell told *USA Weekend* magazine that, out of all the artists out there, he would pick Christina Aguilera as the one people would still be listening to in ten years:

> *"Christina Aguilera. She is an unbelievable talent. Christina's 'Beautiful' is one of the best pop records I have ever heard in my life."*

The Good News

Many people agreed. The album went quadruple platinum, sold more than ten million copies worldwide, and stayed on the *Billboard* charts for two years. The *Stripped* tour that followed was voted the best tour of the year by *Rolling Stone* readers. The single "Beautiful" hit #2 on the *Billboard* Hot 100 and earned Christina a Grammy for Best Female Pop Vocal Performance.

When people saw Christina arrive at the MTV Movie Awards, they had no idea what was in store for them. Then Madonna kissed Britney Spears and Christina during a performance, and it became the kiss heard 'round the world.

In 2004, Christina's album *Stripped* brought her a Grammy Award and many others. But, she also gained a reputation for her fashion and style sense.

When the dust died down, people seemed to realize that *Stripped* actually had a lot of artistic merit. Furthermore, it contained a lot of powerful positive messages about recognizing one's own inner beauty ("Beautiful"), resisting and overcoming abuse ("I'm OK"), and staying true to oneself ("Soar"). The song "Can't Hold Us Down" also spoke about women seizing control, specifically of their own sexuality, and many people claimed it was fired at rap star Eminem, who had trashed Christina in his song "The Real Slim Shady." In the chorus of "Can't Hold Us Down," Christina rallies her female fans:

> *"This is for my girls all around the world*
> *Who've come across a man who don't respect your*
> *worth"*

The positive messages didn't go unnoticed by everyone. Christina received a special award from the Gay and Lesbian Alliance Against Defamation (GLAAD) for showing positive images of gay and transgender people in the video for her single "Beautiful." Perhaps, at the end of the day, Christina was more like her socially conscious role model Madonna after all. The hype around her look and sexual imagery just prevented a lot of people from seeing it—at least at first glance.

Rebirth

Christina didn't stick to her bad-girl phase for long. It seemed that, once she was free to explore that side of herself, she got it out of her system pretty quickly. The black hair and skimpy outfits soon disappeared, and a platinum blond, glam-Hollywood woman emerged. But the new Christina didn't head back into the studio right away. She took her time with her music, *collaborating* with other artists like Missy Elliott, Nelly, and Andrea Bocelli, and lending her voice and image to charity concerts, a get-out-and-vote campaign, and other ventures.

At least part of the reason for Christina's time out of the spotlight was that she was concentrating more on her personal life, particularly her relationship with music executive Jordan Bratman. The couple got engaged in February 2005 and were married a few months later. In an interview, she told AOL Music that she wasn't necessarily looking for life-long love, but it happened, and she just knew it was right:

"I wasn't really looking to get married at all, but over the course of the past five years, Jordan and I have just grown from best friends to wanting to spend the rest of our lives together. When it's the right one, you just know."

Many people attributed Christina's new, softer, more feminine image to finding love, getting married, and settling down. In the interview, Christina said that it's not so much about getting married as finding greater happiness in all aspects of her life. In 2006, she was ready to show that new attitude in her music. In August, she released her third full-length English album, *Back to Basics*.

The two-disc album was another departure from her previous work. Like *Stripped*, it's still urban, but this time it has the flavors of the blues, jazz, and soul music Christina loved growing up. The album debuted at #1 on the *Billboard* 200 chart. None of the singles hit #1, but they have been popular nonetheless. *Back to Basics* is Christina's third multi-platinum-selling album in seven years. It also went #1 in many other countries, setting the stage for Christina's *Back to Basics* World Tour.

The Artist Speaks

Christina felt she grew a lot between her *Stripped* and *Back to Basics* albums, and she told AOL Music that her third album reflects those changes:

"It's a very personal record that touches on a lot of positive things in my life. . . . I had to open myself up to be very vulnerable at times, but I think that makes for a more meaningful record. . . . Sometimes it is difficult to share your innermost feelings with the world, but I think it's an important part of being a real artist and being able to have people relate to you and try to touch them with your music."

Back to Basics also gave Christina the opportunity to take even more control over her music. Many albums are born in the minds of music executives, and the singer must turn their idea into a reality. But Christina was the brain and inspiration behind this album. She had a vision of what she wanted, and then she found the people who could work with her to make it happen. Once again, she was able to write many of the songs, and tracks like "Oh Mother" and "Save Me from Myself" are highly personal stories.

In an MSN Live Chat, Christina talked about how much she loves to write, and how she can be inspired by almost anything:

"Everything inspires me to write songs from the railing I'm leaning on to the clouds in the sky, people in my life, dust on the ground. Everything inspires me. . . . It is always fun for me to write because anything is possible."

Still Christina

For fans who worry that Christina has completely cleaned up and left all the sassy sexiness behind, she says not to be concerned. She may be married and dressing a little classier these days, but Christina claims she'll always have a bit of a wild side. Songs on her *Back to Basics* album like "Still Dirrty" and

Christina is more than looks. She's a talented songwriter and performer who uses music to spread positive messages, especially to young girls. In recognition of her many gifts, *Good Morning America* asked her to be a guest and gave her the chance to sing one of her new songs.

"Nasty Naughty Boy" show the bad girl is still alive and kicking, and some revealing photo shoots following the album's release showed Christina was still willing to bare her skin.

Unlike *Stripped,* however, the album hasn't been consumed by these types of themes, and the songs expressing Christina's gentler side have received greater attention. In the end, critics are beginning to say that there is a lot in Christina Aguilera to admire after all. She may not be the squeaky-clean role model of modesty and virtue that some people would like her to be, but she is a role model in another way; she is a strong woman who can stand up for herself, fight for what she believes in, and always stay true to herself. As far as positive messages in the media go, that's about as good as it gets.

Christina Aguilera has worked hard over the years to help people feel better about themselves. It's something she's worked hard on herself, so she's a living example of what can happen when a person truly believes in herself.

5

The Softer Side of Christina

Since she was just a teenager, Christina Aguilera has been one of the hardest hitting artists in the music industry. She has a powerhouse voice with a powerhouse attitude to back it up. "The little girl with the big voice" is now the glamorous woman with the big career. But as career-minded as Christina has always been, work is far from her only priority.

A Higher Calling

From very early in her life, Christina always saw her music as part of something bigger. First it was a way to escape from the painful realities of her childhood, then it was a way to explore and understand herself; now it is also a way to help others. Christina has always hoped that her songs focusing on surviving abuse, recognizing your own beauty, and fighting for yourself and your beliefs would touch and inspire other people. But she knows that her power goes beyond her words. Christina also wants to put her fame and fortune to good use and the aid of others.

Christina has used her fame and charm to move more than just her career. Several causes are close to her heart. She remains loyal to her hometown, supporting the Women's Center & Shelter of Greater Pittsburgh. After touring the center, she donated $200,000 to it. She raised more money by auctioning off front-row seats and backstage passes to her shows. And her efforts to combat violence against women don't just focus on her hometown; they span the country and the globe. She has contributed to the National Coalition Against Domestic Violence and to Refuge, a British group that cares for women and children affected by domestic violence.

The HIV/AIDS epidemic that is sweeping the globe and destroying populations worldwide has also captured Christina's attention. She has participated in concerts, print ads, and other forums to raise awareness about the epidemic and money for AIDS research. In 2001, she worked with Artists Against AIDS Worldwide to record an "Allstar Tribute" of the Marvin Gaye classic "What's Going On." In the Allstar Tribute version, the song was used to talk about the AIDS epidemic as well as the events of September 11, 2001.

Christina was very proud to be part of the Allstar Tribute and hoped that it would encourage her fans to become involved both in fighting the AIDS epidemic and in other causes. Some of Christina's other causes include animal and wildlife welfare, voter participation, and raising awareness of and funds for the humanitarian crisis in Darfur, a region in western Sudan. In addition, Christina joined the effort to aid Hurricane Katrina victims by donating her wedding gifts to charities, raising money for the disaster relief effort.

Future Goals

Christina now has plenty of interests competing for her time. Nevertheless, she continues to have big career goals as well.

During her early career, some called Christina a diva. If the label ever truly fit her, she's far from that now. Christina is still working hard at her music, but she's also giving back by working on behalf of many charities and worthy causes.

In an MSN Live Chat, she told one fan that she hopes she'll continue to grow and have a career that spans all types of performance:

> *"I think an artist can fit under a few different categories. . . . I thrive on creativity. So in the long run I want to be an all around entertainer. On stage vocalizing, choreography, and doing characters—that's a performer. I love doing it all! One day producing and venturing off into films as well. I want to do as much as I can."*

Christina has not been shy about the fact that she would like to act, but unlike a lot of her peers, she still hasn't jumped into a movie role. She says that plenty of scripts have passed through her hands, and she reads them with interest, but she is waiting for the right thing to come along. She says she doesn't want to play herself, and she doesn't want to play fluff. If she's going to venture into acting, she wants to play a real character with depth, a role she can be challenged by and taken seriously for.

Christina has also recently stated that, although music will always be important to her and she wants to put out future albums, she is beginning to place more emphasis on her personal life. Now that she is married, she thinks she'll soon be ready to take a break from the craziness of making albums, performing, and touring to start a family.

One thing is for certain, whatever Christina chooses to do next, if she approaches it with the same passion, drive, and conviction she has shown thus far in her career, it will be a success. It seems certain that Christina Aguilera will continue to entertain, inspire, and surprise people for years to come as well. And perhaps she'll stir up a little controversy along the way.

Through the years, Christina has developed a confident, no-nonsense attitude. She is self-assured and strong enough to take her music career down the path *she* chooses rather than be led by music industry executives who want to groom her into an image they feel will make the most money. Christina faced this type of handling early in her career, and felt she was being represented differently than she really was. Now she stands up for herself, makes her own decisions about her music, her style, and her image, and inspires people with her strength and daring. She's no longer willing to change for anyone. The words of the hit song, "Beautiful," perhaps best describe her feelings about herself now:

> *"I am beautiful no matter what they say*
> *Words can't bring me down"*

It's a motto she now seems to live by. The song has also become an anthem for many of her fans: Be yourself. Love yourself. Recognize your own beauty. Be your own best friend. Don't let anyone change you. They're lessons Christina has learned throughout her career, and that she now passes on to her fans in her music.

1970s	Hip-hop is born in New York City.
Dec. 18, 1980	Christina Aguilera is born on Staten Island, New York.
1993	Christina becomes a Mouseketeer on *The New Mickey Mouse Club*.
1998	Christina has her first #1 hit with "Genie in a Bottle."
1999	Christina releases her first album, *Christina Aguilera*.
2000	Christina receives her first Grammy nominations and wins for Best New Artist.
	Her Spanish-language album, *Mi Reflejo*, is released.
	She releases a Christmas album, *My Kind of Christmas*.
2001	Christina wins a Latin Grammy Award for *Mi Reflejo*.
	Christina collaborates with Lil' Kim, Mya, and Pink on "Lady Marmalade" for the film *Moulin Rouge!*
	She works with Artists Against AIDS Worldwide.

Christina wins two *Billboard* Latin Music Awards.

Christina receives the World's Best-Selling Latin Female Artist award at the World Music Awards.

2002   *Stripped* is released.

Christina wins a Grammy Award for Best Pop Collaboration with Vocals.

2004   *Glamour* names Christina as Woman of the Year.

Christina wins a Grammy Award for Best Female Pop Vocal Performance.

2005   Christina and Jordan Bratman marry.

2006   *Back to Basics* is released.

Albums

1999	*Christina Aguilera*
2000	*Mi Reflejo*
2000	*My Kind of Christmas*
2002	*Stripped*
2006	*Back to Basics*

Number-One Singles

1998	"Genie in a Bottle"
1999	"What a Girl Wants"
2000	"Come on Over Baby (All I Want Is You)"
2001	"Nobody Wants to Be Lonely" (with Ricky Martin)
2001	"Lady Marmalade" (with Lil' Kim, Mya, and Pink)
2002	"Beautiful"

DVDs

1999	*Genie Gets Her Wish*
2000	*My Reflection*

2003 *Fighter/Beautiful*

2004 *Stripped—Live in the UK*

2005 *Christina Aguilera: Music Box Biographical Collection*

Select Awards and Recognitions

1999 Ivor Novello Award: International Hit of the Year ("Genie in a Bottle"); *Ladies' Home Journal*: Top 10 Most Fascinating Women of 1999.

2000 ALMA Award: Best New Artist; Amigo Award: Best International Newcomer; *Billboard* Music Award: Female Artist of the Year; *Entertainment Weekly* Award: Best Websites of the 21st Century; Grammy Awards: Best New Artist; *Latina* Magazine: 2000 Entertainer of the Year; *Maxim* Women of the Year Award: Best International Female Singer; Starlight Award: Outstanding Humanitarian Contribution; *Teen Magazine*: Best Girl-Power Song ("What a Girl Wants), Best Female Artist; World Music Award: World's Best-Selling Female New Artist.

2001 *Billboard* Latin Music Award: Best Pop Album of the Year, Female, and Best Pop Album of the Year, New Artist (both for *Mi Reflejo*); Latin Grammy Award: Best Female Pop Vocal Album (*Mi Reflejo*); Lo Nuestro Award: Best New Artist, Best Female

Artist of the Year; World Music Award: World's Best-Selling Latin Female Artist.

2002 Grammy Awards: Best Pop Collaboration with Vocals ("Lady Marmalade").

2003 *Blender*: Woman of the Year; *Cove* Magazine: No. 1 Best Pop Vocalist; GLAAD Media Awards: Special Recognition Award; MOBO Awards: Best Video (*Dirrty*); MTV Europe Music Awards: Best Female; *Sugar* Magazine: Inspirational Girls Top 100; *Top of the Pops* Awards: Singer of the Year.

2004 *Glamour* Women of the Year Awards: Woman of the Year; Grammy Awards: Best Female Pop Vocal Performance ("Beautiful"); Groovevolt Music & Fashion Awards: Album of the Year (*Stripped*), Song of the Year ("Beautiful"), Video of the Year (*Beautiful*), Most Fashionable Music Video (*Can't Hold Us Down*); *Rolling Stone* Music Awards: Best Female Performer—Readers' Pick, Best Tour—Readers' Pick (*Justified* and *Stripped*).

2006 MTV Europe Music Awards: Best Female; Rolling Stone Music Awards: Best Female Performer—Readers' Pick, Best R&B Artist—Readers' Pick.

2007 Grammy Awards: Best Female Pop Vocal Performance ("Ain't No Other Man").

Books

Chang, Jeff. *Can't Stop Won't Stop: A History of the Hip-Hop Generation*. New York: Picador, 2005.

Gabriel, Jan. *Backstage Pass: Christina Aguilera*. New York: Scholastic, 2000.

Golden, Anna Louise. *Christina Aguilera*. New York: St. Martins, 2001.

Granados, Christine. *Christina Aguilera*. Hoskessin, Del.: Mitchell Lane, 2004.

Joseph, Paul, Tamara L. Britton, and Lori Kinstad Pupeza. *Christina Aguilera*. Edina, Minn.: ABDO, 2000.

Korman, Susan. *Christina Aguilera*. New York: Chelsea House, 2002.

Light, Alan (ed.). *The Vibe History of Hip Hop*. New York: Three Rivers Press, 1999.

Robb, Jackie. *Christina Aguilera*. London, UK: Boxtree Ltd., 2000.

Talmadge, Morgan. *Christina Aguilera*. New York: Rosen, 2001.

Web Sites

Christina Aguilera on My Space
www.myspace.com/christinaaguilera

Christina Aguilera Official Web site
www.christinaaguilera.com

Christina Aguilera Tribute Site
www.christina-a.net

Glossary

blues—A musical style that developed from African American folk songs in the early 20th century and consisting of primarily sad songs.

collaborating—Working with others on a project.

defiant—Deliberately and openly disobedient.

demo—A recorded sample of music produced to promote something.

diva—An extremely arrogant or glamorous woman, especially an actress or singer.

diversity—Ethnic, socioeconomic, and gender variety within a group, society, or institution.

empowered—Being given power or authority.

hype—Greatly exaggerated publicity.

jazz—A music style that originated among blacks in New Orleans during the late nineteenth century, and that is known for its syncopated rhythms and improvisation.

mainstream—The ideas, actions, and values that are most widely accepted by a group or society.

persona—The image of character and personality that someone wants to show the outside world.

platinum—A designation that a recording has sold 1 million units.

R&B—Rhythm and blues; a style of music originally developed by African American musicians that combines elements of jazz and blues.

soul—A style of African American music that has a strong emotional quality and what is drawn from gospel and rhythm and blues music.

Index

About the Author

MaryJo Lemmens is a children's nonfiction writer who lives in Toronto, Ontario, Canada's largest city. Before moving to Toronto, she lived in the United States and South Africa. She received her bachelor's degree from Smith College in Northampton, Massachusetts. She has written numerous publications for young people.

Picture Credits

Harris, Glenn / PR Photos: front cover, pp. 28, 33, 38, 42, 44
Hatcher, Chris / PR Photos: pp. 2, 8, 51
iStockphoto: p. 11
    Cetkovic, Jovana: p. 12
    Heymans, Dagmar: p. 18
Mayer, Janet / PR Photos: pp. 46, 48
PR Photos: pp. 14, 16
Thompson, Terry / PR Photos: pp. 23, 28, 31
Walck, Tom / PR Photos: p. 37
Wild 1 / PR Photos: p. 21

To the best knowledge of the publisher, all other images are in the public domain. If any image has been inadvertently uncredited, please notify Harding House Publishing Service, Vestal, New York 13850, so that rectification can be made for future printings.